ECHOES INTERTWINED

*PARABLES, LESSONS AND **GOD** WHISPERS*

john g. adams

Copyright © 2021 by John G. Adams

All rights reserved. No part of this book may be reproduced, distributed or transmitted in any form or by any means, including photocopying, recording, or other electronic or mechanical methods, without the prior written permission of the publisher, except in the case of brief quotations embodied in critical reviews and certain other noncommercial uses permitted by copyright law.

Holy Bible - New International Version® (unless otherwise noted) www.biblegateway.com © 1995-2020, The Zondervan Corporation. All Rights Reserved.

ISBN: 9798739289698 (print only)

Moments of Sabbath artwork - Julie Teal
Cover art : Rachel Merritt - www.raemerritt.com

Special Thanks to Jules, Kristen, Cindy, Marni and Rachel for sharing the visions that play in my head and helping to focus the lens.

If you enjoy *Tapestry Unraveled*, I'd love to hear from you. Your thoughts matter.

Visit *www.LiftedKeys.com* for more stories, devotionals and inspiration; words entrusted to lift hearts and warm souls.

www.LiftedKeys.com

To Cheryl
For loving me 99% of the time
and renewing my contract
each December in spite of the lingering 1%.

To Natalie
For bringing the love of music to the world
and making it a better place
just by being in it.

Foreword

Despite having known John for 25 years, his writing has given me a much more intimate glimpse into who he really is. These devotional entries are broad, rich, applicable, and humbly offered by one who laughs at himself. John includes Biblical references with each devotional – some familiar to many of us, others a bit more obscure and refreshingly eye-opening (Ex: "Heaping Coals").

John's writing is prompted by his Spirit-thirsty heart and fueled by inspiration. His genuine relationship with God invites the reader to dig deeper, as well. Some devotionals are encouraging and strengthening... others caused me to say "ouch." All are personal and authentic.

Finally, in my enthusiasm to read John's book, I did so in one sitting. I realized that, although I was blessed by the variety of spiritual insights it contains, my haste robbed me of the privilege of letting each message soak into my heart and mind. My second reading brought more personal meaning and application. I challenge you to read and savor each entry.

Steve Purdy - Pastor

The Lord came and stood there, calling as at the other times, "Samuel! Samuel!"

Then Samuel said, "Speak, for your servant is listening."

And the Lord said to Samuel: "See, I am about to do something in Israel that will make the ears of everyone who hears about it tingle."

1 Samuel 3:10-11

A kind gesture, a gift of an empty journal, pages yearning for scribblings of thoughts and dreams, a greater gift than soft gray leather could encompass. Pages of mundane frustrations led to written dialogue of the tug-of-war that rages in distant corners of my cranium. Incoherent ramblings gave license to question the "why-s" and "how-s" prompting prayer, study, and seeking wisdom from the Almighty, who not only holds the key to such questions, but also created the answers and my desire to seek them.

A silent church awaits a heart-wrenching melody. Fingers press ivory keys, felt hammers strike metal strings, music emerges through wood and iron - in Echoes. In the same way, our prayers, whether joyful or painful, journey through flesh and bone, breath and heartbeat to the heavenly realms - in Echoes. Yet unlike mimicked sounds bouncing off castle walls, prayers return in whispers, gentle (and not so gentle) nudges and God's unique sense of humor - in Echoes.

Music flows through my fingers as lifeblood spilling over alternating ebony and ivory, intermingling with the precious blood of Christ. Melody and harmony in tune with the Almighty. Echoes Intertwined.

Entertainer of Angels

I was asked to help in a small part of a particular project. In the midst, as I balanced on a ladder with a tool in each hand, I realized my "small" part had grown into the lion's share. Not that I minded or did not expect it, but the absurdity struck me as funny. I heard a heavenly giggle. There I go, entertaining angels again.

The origin of the phrase "entertaining angels" is from the book of Hebrews:

"Do not neglect to show hospitality to strangers, for by this some have entertained angels without knowing it." Hebrews 13:2 NASB

Be hospitable to strangers for you may have welcomed angels without knowing it. I get that, but I have always enjoyed thinking the "entertaining" part was making angels laugh. One of my favorite images of Jesus is the one commonly called "laughing Jesus". Most of the images we have, in word or on canvas, is of a man, focused in prayer, intensely imparting wisdom, compassionate toward the sick, weeping at the death of a friend, or the agony of His own earthly death. However, this image is Jesus laughing, not just a chuckle, but also a hearty, belly laugh.

We do not read much about Him laughing. He was a kid so there was running, playing and undoubtedly laughter. He must have laughed as the children came to Him. He probably laughed at Peter when he would say something bold, often speaking before thinking. And I'm sure He laughs when I tell Him about "my" plans.

Oh, Jesus laughs all right!

I feel Him poke me in the ribs at times when I fail to recognize a bit of irony that He placed before me. Moreover, I am sure I make Him laugh, after all, I am created in His image, and I laugh at myself all the time. I imagine the angels rolling their eyes at me and saying, "OK, who gets to fly with him today?"

I am glad God has a sense of humor. So I guess I am an entertainer of angels after all.

Gospel in the Butterflies

"Walking in the garden in the cool of the day" was something the Lord did according to Genesis.

Similarly, I was walking in the relative 91 degree "cool" of a Texas July evening when a song ran through my head about "ridiculous grace," and as ridiculous as it seems, I have been blessed by that grace. Pondering why, I saw the silhouette of a pair of butterflies looking for a place to park for the night. They settled on their respective spots, closed their wings and faded into the branches of a towering live oak tree. These two seemingly insignificant insects disappeared into the shelter of this huge tree. Two beautiful creatures, never to be seen by anyone but me in that exact moment, were taken care of. They will go on to flutter and live their lives, completely unnoticed.

"Consider the ravens: They do not sow or reap, they have no storeroom or barn; yet God feeds them. And how much more valuable you are than birds!" Luke 12:24

These small butterflies were beautiful, fed and protected. How much more will we be cared for? Why worry about riches? *"The pagans chase after these things." Luke 12:30*

The balance between success at your job and chasing riches is difficult to maintain. There is a passage in Proverbs 30 that I rely on often.

"Keep falsehood and lies far from me; give me neither poverty nor riches, but give me only my daily bread. Otherwise, I may have too much and disown you and say, 'Who is the Lord?' Or I may become poor and steal, and so dishonor the name of my God." Proverbs 30:8-9

I think I could handle a little more than I need and it is hard not to see what others have and dream. Then I come home to our little house on our little piece of Texas, to my wife of 30+ years, our daughter, two dogs, and just enough to keep our pile of bills at bay. I certainly have more than enough.

Not an Empty Vessel

The nurse attempted a blood draw, but my veins were not cooperating. For those of us "hard stick" people, it can be a challenge. After a few dry holes, they brought in the "one stick" nurse (I wish they had started with her). I joked that there was blood in there somewhere. She replied, "You are not an empty vessel". Right there, in the midst of doctors, needles, jars of cotton balls and tongue depressors, I felt convicted. I truly was not an empty vessel. Thoughts rushed into my head of past failures, propensity to fail, and the other junk I can never seem to scrape out of my "vessel".

Vessel - a large ship, a container, a tubular channel by which life-giving blood flows. Not just physically restricted by the remnants of past barbecue and chicken fried steaks, but spiritually clogged with crusty deposits of weakness and faithlessness. Leftover muck taking up space that should instead be filled with God's peace and love. With a heavy heart, I prayed for a cleansing of the crud.

I considered the nurses words again. "You are not an empty vessel." Maybe there was more in there than I thought. My mind always leads with the negative; just a way to stay humble, or evil festering another deception, telling me I am not worthy of Jesus' sacrifice. Of course, I am not worthy. That is why He had to go to the cross, because He loves me like no other.

"Blessed is the one whose transgressions are forgiven, whose sins are covered." Psalm 32:1

Our sins are covered by His mercy, never to be seen again. Yes, there may be crud in my vessel, but it is covered by grace, by the blood of Jesus. Amen.

Not an empty vessel indeed.

Seasons

"There is a time for everything, and a season for every activity under the heavens." Ecclesiastes 3:1

    Life is a series of seasons. In South Texas, we have two seasons: long summer and short winter, green and then brown. Autumn in Northern Virginia yielded the brilliant colors of the Shenandoah Valley: reds, yellows, gold, and everything in between.
    Business runs in seasons as well. As an earthwork contractor, long summers yield prosperity while an extended rainy fall results in the opposite. If you endure the bad weather, the sun will break through again.

"a time to weep and a time to laugh, a time to mourn and a time to dance" Ecclesiastes 3:4 NIV

    We live our lives through seasons of ups and downs, fulfillment and emptiness, joy and sorrow. If you endure the bad weather, the sun will break through again.

"a time to be silent and a time to speak"
Ecclesiastes 3:7

A time to fill a page and a time to leave it empty. I have had seasons when new songs flowed like God's abundant grace: poignant or fun, somber or lively, soul searching or soul refreshing and others when I stare at a blank page, wondering why my muse is disinterested. Some seasons are frustrating.

"Very truly I tell you, unless a kernel of wheat falls to the ground and dies, it remains only a single seed. But if it dies, it produces many seeds." John 12:24

So we must pass through difficult seasons to prepare for the next. A surprise gift of an empty journal made it to my door and I took it as a push to write again; a new season. At first it was every day, then whenever I needed to get something off my chest, even if it was just for me. I found that pouring out a struggle on paper resulted in an answer, even if only pray and wait. Most pages were filled with the mundane, not suitable for public consumption, let alone interest; however, every once in a while, a thought would pop up that needed more pondering. Mix in patience, Bible time and a touch of God granted wisdom and parables began to take shape. Scribbling thoughts allows space to blow off steam, mumble, grumble and listen for heavenly whispers. It is also an account of where I was and where I am. Looking back I realize that some seasons were simply lessons waiting to be learned.

Pushed Out of the Nest

On a particularly stress filled day, being pulled in different directions, each wheel was trying to be the squeakiest, vying for a limited amount of grease. As fires settled to embers, I needed some time with the Master so I broke away for a walk.

> *"Likewise the Spirit helps us in our weakness; for we do not know how to pray as we ought, but that very Spirit intercedes for us with sighs too deep for words."* Romans 8:26 ESV

That is good; I had run out of things to pray.

My empty gaze moved skyward to see a hawk; its silhouette offset against a light blue sky and soft white clouds, circling effortlessly on the gentle breeze. Its pattern grew wider and further away until it was out of my view. In the time I watched, it only flapped a wing once. The breeze was doing all the work.

The serenity brought peace to a weary mind, yet being carried by the breath of God became a more poignant interpretation. Why was this hawk circling? Looking for food? Looking for a mate? Or maybe just enjoying the fact that it could fly. The hawk was doing what it was made to do with most of the flight being aided by the Grace of God. Now I am sure there was some work involved to catch the breeze, then only a slight shift of its wings.

Majestic in flight but that was not always the case. Once upon a time, the hawk snuggled in a warm nest, peering over the edge. Not until it was pushed, with the ground and certain death quickly approaching, did its God given talent take over, and it flew.

Facing a new challenge, we are content to peek over the edge of the nest, hoping to stay in our comfort zone. We do not always take to flying; it requires multiple attempts, practice, and hard work to find the cool breeze that will carry us along our way. As long as we focus on our little corner of the nest, we fail to see the bigger sky that is waiting for us. Created to fly, we persevere through the headwinds, finding the cool breeze of God's Grace carrying us higher and further than we could dream.

We simply need to shift our wings to let God's Grace take us where He wills.

Born Sleeping

Recently, a colleague and his wife suddenly lost their unborn child. We work in separate departments and I did not know them well enough to know they were pregnant. Whether it was empathy or sympathy, the loss hit me hard.

When Jesus went to Bethany as His dear friend Lazarus had died, the Gospel says that He *"groaned in the spirit and was troubled"* and *"He wept." John 11:33 and 11:35* . Jesus was not weeping because Lazarus had "fallen asleep." Jesus knew He would call Lazarus out of the grave that day. No, I believe He wept out of compassion because of the pain that the family was feeling.

I have never had to bear the loss of a child so I cannot begin to know what they are going through.

Feeling the need to send some words of comfort but finding none, I sent a link to a song by Selah called *I Will Carry You (Audrey's Song)*, a beautiful song about a mother forever carrying a child that had earned its angel wings and how Jesus is carrying them both. I pray that Jesus can use it to help soothe their aching hearts.

Looking for answers to the "whys", some lyrics came to mind. Something like:

Searching for the right words to say
Angel babies needed one more to play
Angel mommies needed one more to hold
Angel grandmas needed one more to hear their stories told.
Trusting her to the One that really knows her,
Jesus needed to hold her closer.

As a song was forming, my heart was breaking so hard, I had to stop. As the day pressed on, more lyrics leaked out like teardrops. Then I got a call from my child. I was even more grateful for the blessing that she is.

Later, the angel baby's parents posted her birth announcement. It said she was "born sleeping" and that she was loved, wanted, and missed.

What a beautiful thought. Imagine sleeping in the arms of Jesus.

We grieve because we have to wait to hold the ones we love that have gone on ahead. Until then, Jesus will be holding them closely. He is certainly holding this precious little one, until her parents see her again, skipping along and playing with the other angel babies.

The cloudy skies of this life do fade in the Light of Eternity.

The Heavens Opened Up

"And Jesus, when He had been baptized, went up straightway out of the water. And lo, the heavens were opened unto Him, and He saw the Spirit of God descending like a dove and lighting upon Him." Matthew 3:16 KJV

Baptism of Our Lord Sunday; another chance to lead worship. Having experienced some heavenly direction in song selection, I was excited about the day, yet on these mornings there are nerves. Whether performance anxiety or fear of my hands and voice failing today's calling, I don't know. Probably both.

I walked out, breathing in the crisp, cool air of a January morning; hints of a glorious sunrise and a single star peering out. Arriving at church, I see the same star and another beside it, Mars, Venus, perhaps, but a welcome sight. I had written a song about no shining star to follow. Then through the quiet morning light, beyond the shadows of power lines, pecan trees and the warm glow of church windows, the star appeared.

The Pastor's message was about how the heavens seemed to close when sin entered the garden of Eden and reopened when Jesus emerged from the Jordan River, freshly baptized. The music began well and my voice was surprisingly warm for a cool morning. Then the "froggies" showed up in my throat, my mind began to wander and my hands were sure to follow. The pastor was teaching the children about the baptismal font. I took a drink of water mixed with a touch of lemon, and it soothed my vocal chords and my soul. It struck me as a baptism of sorts.

In baptism, Jesus reopened heaven to us. We should look for heaven's opening at every turn. I fail to see it as often as I should. I need a gentle (and sometimes NOT so gentle) nudge.

Our opening hymn was *Great is Thy Faithfulness*.

> "Morning by morning new mercies I see.
> All I have needed Thy hands have provided.
> Great is Thy faithfulness Lord unto me."

Indeed.

The heavens opened up this morning. I was re-baptized and refreshed.

Borrowing Some Shade

How often do you hear of someone settling down near where they grew up? I, too, am one of those. After marrying my sweet bride, I hauled her out of South Texas to the Blue Ridge Mountains of Northern Virginia for a time, eventually moving back home to raise our family. After a few employers came and went, I ended up at an office that was close to where my father spent the majority of his career. I drive by often and still feel a kinship with memories of "bring your son to work" days.

In the midst of the pandemic, open dining rooms were hard to come by. Most of the time, I would brown bag it or hit the drive-thru, then look for a cool spot to park and "dine." This day, I drove through my father's former work area and found a nice space, cooled by the far-reaching branches of an ancient oak tree.

This particular place is parking for a local university, currently empty. Security personnel in golf carts passed by slowly, checking up on me. Had they stopped, my reasoning would be, "I was just borrowing some shade from my father." He had put in enough time here to buy me at least half an hour of peace. Feeling closer to my earthly father made me appreciate the other things I "borrow" from him: integrity, intelligence, work ethic and most importantly faith; long reaching branches that render shade when other forces burn like a South Texas afternoon.

His branches were enveloped by those of our Heavenly Father, providing shade to my father's endeavors, which in turn shade mine. Had my father not appreciated heavenly shade, he could not have shown me how to myself. Thanks Dad.

Forever grateful for the strong, ancient branches that grant their shade for those who seek them and rest in their cooling peace.

Orchestrate

Orchestrate :
To arrange the elements of a situation to produce the desired effect. Mostly used in a musical sense.

    Do you ever marvel when things fall into place, especially after long nights of worrisome sleep? How about when they do not come together, but later, upon reflection, the pieces formed a completely different picture?
    I have a dear friend who was broken. Her marriage was over; new job; new house; new situations. I had not seen her in years, but a business meeting placed us in the same place at the same time. She was just going through the motions, one day at a time. I listened, tried to understand, offered a kind hug or two and we went our separate ways. On the drive home, my heart was breaking for her and lyrics began to pour out, praying Jesus would hold her together until the broken pieces fell into place.
    Fast forward, she rekindled a flame from her younger years, got married and her life is great. I gave her a copy of my old lyrics as a wedding gift.

The broken pieces were finally in place.

"For I know the plans I have for you," declares the Lord, "plans to prosper you and not to harm you, plans to give you hope and a future." Jeremiah 29:11

Orchestrated? Definitely.

We consider an orchestra as a very large group of musicians. A smaller group is referred to as an ensemble.

The music, whether for a large or small group is still orchestrated.

I feel like a member of an ensemble being orchestrated by the Great Director. Yet instead of having the full score where I can peek at the last page, I am being directed to sight read as the notes come along. God says the grand finale is written, but we are not prepared for it yet.

The first movement of that symphony was tense, but ended beautifully. The measures in-between were the hard ones. Our lives go through many measures, some minor, some major, some diminished, some sustained. God directs the melodies of our heart. We just have to listen and stay in tune.

One day, the Grand Finale will be amazing.

Keep Ahead of the Old Man

When work is to be done at my father-in-law's place, taking a break or quitting early is not an option when an 80+ year old is outworking you. The further "18" is in the rear view mirror, the less time it takes to be reminded that I am not 18 anymore.

When faced with a "honey-do" or "sonny-do" list, I tackle "have-to's" before "want-to's", hoping to finish before I run out of juice and "the old man" in me catches up.

"Lie not one to another, seeing that ye have put off the old man with his deeds; and have put on the new man, which is renewed in knowledge after the image of him that created him." Colossians 3:8-10 KJV

The "old man" is your old self, your old ways, which you put away when you put on your new self, the image of the Creator. The thought of THAT "old man" catching up is devastating.

"I have been crucified with Christ and I no longer live, but Christ lives in me. The life I now live in the body, I live by faith in the Son of God, who loved me and gave himself for me." Galatians 2:20

The "old man" was nailed to the cross with Jesus. The old ways are gone; easy enough to say until triggers of the old reappear, and not surprisingly, at our weakest moments. Temptation is good at that. Tired, hurting, frustrated, depressed, and our sin of choice presents itself as an escape from whatever we are going through.

"And lead us not into temptation, but deliver us from the evil one." Matthew 6:13

Pray for wisdom to see temptation for what it is and for the strength to endure it. Keep one step ahead of the old man. If the old man sneaks up on you, work harder to regain the lead. Do whatever it takes. Walk away, pray, sing, turn around and run.

"No temptation has overtaken you except what is common to mankind. And God is faithful; he will not let you be tempted beyond what you can bear. But when you are tempted, he will also provide a way out so that you can endure it."
1 Corinthians 10:13

God always provides a way out, we just have to recognize it and use it.

I pray that I may have the vision to see what is coming, the strength to choose the way out, and the wisdom to know whether to walk or run.

I pray the same for you.

40 Days at the Feet of Jesus

40 days and 40 nights did it rain children. Que the *School House Rock*. If you do not know what that is, look it up. They snuck some lernin' into our Saturday morning cartoons.

It rained on Noah 40 days. Moses wandered the desert for 40 years. Jesus spent 40 days in the wilderness. The number 40 appears in scripture 146 times.

"When Moses received God's laws, he was on the mountain for 40 days" – Exodus 24:18 and again in Exodus 34:28.

Goliath stood and chided the Israelites 40 days before David faced him. The number 40 represents a time of testing or trial.

The Lenten season is based on 40 days. Ash Wednesday is 46 days before Easter; 40 days with 6 Sundays interspersed. Lent traditionally is a time to give something up in lieu of complete fasting. A friend tried to give up his virginity for Lent, a clever pickup line, though ineffective. Instead of giving something up for Lent, try adding something: either starting a healthy habit, or serving others. I wonder how many truly treat Lent as it was intended instead of just an excuse to have Mardi Gras.

Lent began as a time of reflection and repentance in preparation and remembrance of Jesus' sacrifice on the cross and His rising three days later. *Hallelujah*. Instead of giving up chocolate (which is never a good idea) or simply eating fish on Fridays, why not take time to examine ourselves from the inside?

What if, instead, we gave up hatred, resentment and jealousy? What if we offered long overdue forgiveness and pray for those who always seem to be in our way? Wow, those are some noble "preacher words". If only I could live them as easily as I wrote them.

Perhaps this Lenten season I will admit my rough edges and see there is still much work to do inside and out. What about spending more time drawing nearer to God and allowing Him to mold me? What if it did not end after just 40 days?

"Search me, O God, and know my heart: try me, and know my thoughts: And see if there be any wicked way in me, and lead me in the way everlasting." Psalm 139:23-24 KJV

There is work to do. Lord, help me find and refine my rough edges.

"Wash me, and I will be whiter than snow." Psalm 51:7

Amen...

Watermarks

    Morning commute, sun is shining, a crisp breeze outside; taking the long way to work. Left to myself, my prayer time wavered and I got lost in the thoughts of the upcoming day. Turning up the road to a blast of sunlight in my eyes, adjusting my visor, I noticed dried water spots on my windshield. The sun showed clearly through the glass, but exposed the remnants of the rain sprinkles from the previous night; a whisper of a lesson. What kind of metaphor could the spots be? Long forgotten teardrops? God encompassing the tears of the hurting? Maybe just wait for "the rest of the story" (thank you *Paul Harvey* for your brilliance).
    The day began with a series of unfortunate disappointments, each one like a water spot shielding me from a clear mind and a loving heart. New spots were compounding old dirt from previous battles. I needed a squeegee for my soul to clear the grime of old unforgiven wrongs on top of sheer apathy. I needed to forgive, but angry and hurt inside, I could not pray with an honest heart. I asked God to help me forgive.

Jesus said:

"You have heard that it was said, 'You shall love your neighbor and hate your enemy.' But I say to you, love your enemies, bless those who curse you, do good to those who hate you, and pray for those who spitefully use you and persecute you, that you may be sons of your Father in heaven; for He makes His sun rise on the evil and on the good, and sends rain on the just and on the unjust." Matthew 5:43-45 KJV

I prayed they would be blessed. It is all I had and all I could do.

My encounters went much smoother later in the day. Maybe there was more to the spots than just spots. Maybe the lesson was about "watermarks."

Watermark – a faint design made in paper or currency during manufacture that is visible when held against the light and typically identifies the maker. When dirt is scraped away (sometimes painfully), the watermarks can identify our Maker when held to the light.

Peter tried to hide out in the courtyard the night Jesus was arrested,

"After a little while, those standing there went up to Peter and said, 'Surely you are one of them; your accent gives you away.'" Matthew 26:73

Does our speech expose that we belong to Jesus? When held to the light, do we reflect the watermark of our Maker or are there just spots? I pray that we could all be a true reflection of Jesus.

Pie

Entitlement is a word that gets passed around a lot, meaning to bestow a title on someone, so to be "entitled" means you have claim to some privilege. "Entitlement" has become the belief you have the right to a privilege. If you do not, it should be "falsely perceived entitlement" but that does not play well on television.

I too have had seasons when the big green monster of jealousy reared its ugly head; others being promoted around me (some deservedly, some not so much) standing like prison walls, keeping me in my place. Everyone seemed to be getting a healthy serving of pie. I like pie, where is my pie?

Hungering for pie that I believed I deserved, I got my pie, but it was "humble" pie. It was bitter and stuck in my throat; no glass of self-serving, ego stroking "milk" could wash away that taste and I pouted like a two year old. Then grace or wisdom (or some of both) infused my thoughts.

"Then Jesus was led by the Spirit into the wilderness to be tempted by the devil. Again, the devil took him to a very high mountain and *showed him all the kingdoms of the world and their splendor. "All this I will give you," he said, "if you will bow down and worship me." Jesus said to him, "Away from me, Satan! For it is written: 'Worship the Lord your God, and serve him only.'" Matthew 4:1,8-11*

    Jesus was offered the entire pie but chose to serve God. When Jesus gathered for the Passover meal, instead of accepting the crown He deserved, He washed the disciples' feet. On the cross, He could have saved Himself but He chose to take my sin on His back and leave it in the grave. Certainly not the "pie" He deserved.

    Now in no means do I equate my minor struggles with what Jesus went through. The hint of comparison makes my little pity party rather embarrassing. Jesus did not have to endure beatings, crown of thorns on His head, nails in His hands and feet, and earthly death, but He chose to, to do His Fathers will, all for me and you. I am grateful.

    So where does that leave me? The tasks I completed (throwing pride aside) were an opportunity to wash feet. Not a pleasant task, but a worthy one, with Jesus as an example. Does a worthy task entitle me to a privilege? Perhaps my slice of pie is sitting at Jesus' feet, singing the praise He is so richly entitled to, not only with every earthly breath, but every eternal breath as well.

    Now that's a good piece of pie.

Consider the Bluebonnets

The news of a friend's father earning his angel wings left me with a heavy heart, yet I forged through the day. Returning home, troubles of the day blowing out of my truck windows, the smell of the city faded into the aromas of cattle pastures with new baby calves dancing in the high grass. I tried to scrape the funk off like mud on my boots, to no avail. Expending all my energy to kiss my wife at the back door (okay, that wasn't too hard), I took care of a few chores and helped with dinner, but the burdens lingered on. I sat on the front porch, my shoulders heavy and my eyes downward as if to be bowing my head seeking God's comfort. There, directly in my vision, in the pale light of the evening, was a small bluebonnet. Not the "postcard" version of the brilliant blue South Texas variety, but a new sprout, with a faded color between blue and purple, the "Charlie Brown Christmas Tree" of bluebonnets. It caught my eye, even though surrounded by the brilliant reds of Indian Paint Brushes and the bright white of thistle flowers.

"Consider how the wild flowers grow. They do not labor or spin. Yet I tell you, not even Solomon in all his splendor was dressed like one of these. If that is how God clothes the grass of the field, which is here today, and tomorrow is thrown into the fire, how much more will he clothe you—you of little faith!" Luke 12:27-28

Then a gentle whisper, *"I've Got This."*
I could breathe again. I spent the rest of the evening enjoying the best things in my life.
When I get a heavenly whisper, there is a sense of understanding, a lesson that hopefully makes it to pen and paper. However, this time, the whisper was just a whisper, or so I thought. In preparing for Easter, I was reading about Jesus' last minutes on the cross. As Jesus was breathing His last breaths, He cried out:

"Into your hands I commit my spirit; deliver me, Lord, my faithful God." Psalm 31:5

As with my troubles (which are certainly of no comparison), God said, *"I've Got This."* The burden of pain and torture, and the weight of my sin on His shoulders was lifted by His heavenly Father. He breathed His final earthly breath and a new heavenly breath. *Hallelujah.*
The next time you stop on the roadside on a South Texas afternoon to take in the beauty of a field, painted with the velvety hue of bluebonnets, consider the least of the flowers. God hand-painted each of them as well. How much more does He care for us?
Take the time to hear Him whisper, *"I've Got This"*.

Keep the Change

Change may seem inevitable, but not all change. As we age, our eyes grow weak while hopefully, our spiritual eyes grow stronger in faith and wisdom. For some of us, our hair changes, either turning gray or turning loose. Our hearts change as seasons of emptiness and fulfillment run their courses, but what about our soul?

"In those days John the Baptist came, preaching in the wilderness of Judea and saying, 'Repent, for the kingdom of heaven has come near. I baptize you with water for repentance. But after me comes one who is more powerful than I, whose sandals I am not worthy to carry. He will baptize you with the Holy Spirit and fire.' " Matthew 3:1 and 11

To repent is showing remorse for something you have done, or have not done, but true repentance is feeling enough regret to change directions, never to go back again, though often not fully changed, but a work in progress. John baptized with water for repentance and forgiveness. The baptized rose from the Jordan

River refreshed and clean, but truly changed? Or just changed for now.

I had a friend who was excited about being baptized in his church, and rightfully so. The day was coming up as soon as the church could schedule it. At lunch that day, I flicked water at him and said, "Why wait?" He was disgusted with me for making light of it, but I did not intend to cheapen the event. I believe that if you are ready to be clean and baptized inside, do not wait for someone to work you into their schedule, make the change now. The church ceremony is simply a celebration of the change in you that has already happened. It is not just taking a dunk in the baptismal tank, (or just a sprinkle on the head), it is about really changing and "keeping the change".

"Repent, then, and turn to God, so that your sins may be wiped out, that times of refreshing may come from the Lord." Acts 3:19

Even though it seems everything changes, there is One who never changes.

"Every good and perfect gift is from above, coming down from the Father of the heavenly lights, who does not change like shifting shadows." James 1:17

Our heavenly Father loves us. That does not change. What should change is our hearts, to love others as He loves us. When that change happens, "Keep the Change."

Green Thumb

    My hands have been known to find their way around piano keys and guitar strings. They have worn the black of oil changes, the grey of a hammer and nails, the purple of plumber's glue, and all the colors of the rainbow in oil paint, craft paint and house paint. However, of all the colors these ten digits have been, a green thumb is not one of them. It is a good thing my dear bride inherited that from her father, because I cannot even keep cactus alive.
    My in-laws' yard is a mixture of grand live oak trees and a multitude of towering pine trees. A family spring ritual is gathering baby pine tree sprouts and cultivating them until they can survive on their own. Walking slowly through the yard looking for little sprigs peeking through brown pine needles, fallen leaves and the occasional pine cone, my wife takes one step and finds at least half a dozen "tree-lets". My in-laws were discovering them left and right, I think the dog even dug up a few, but me? I am finding weeds, grass, and the beginnings of wildflowers. Then I saw my first one; barely an inch tall but a tree in the making all the same. I looked at the

towering 40 foot tall pines and my conscience wandered. Pine seeds that floated to the ground last fall covered by discarded leaves of the winter season are now sprouts breaking out from their dormant state, surrounded by magnificent trees, result of years of care, both humanly and Godly. How much more does a kind word or a loving gesture seem to go unnoticed, like those seeds, buried under the hurried pace of our daily lives.

"Sow your seed in the morning, and at evening let your hands not be idle, for you do not know which will succeed, whether this or that, or whether both will do equally well." Ecclesiastes 11:6

A seed planted may take root or be consumed by a passing bird seeking nourishment. So too, an offered prayer or shoulder to cry on may take root, providing spiritual nourishment.

"Let us not become weary in doing good, for at the proper time we will reap a harvest if we do not give up." Galatians 6:9

We may never know the change we made in a life until we meet in heaven and hear the story. Occasionally, I have seen a sprout from a seed sown, either an answered prayer or a heart moved by a melody. Maybe I have a green thumb after all.

Count the Cost

Much of my time is spent compiling feasibility studies, a fancy phrase for a budget; yet even if a project is deemed feasible, the client usually requires multiple proposals to ensure the best price. If my efforts yield any fruit at all, it is a "thank you" and a seat at the table to compete for the project. Though at times discouraging, client relationships have great value and I cannot fault the client for asking for help with his due diligence. It is biblical after all.

"Suppose one of you wants to build a tower. Won't you first sit down and estimate the cost to see if you have enough money to complete it? For if you lay the foundation and are not able to finish it, everyone who sees it will ridicule you, saying, 'This person began to build and wasn't able to finish.' " Luke 14:28-30

This parable is about counting the cost, but Jesus told the story as it relates to the cost of following Him. Much more than hanging around to see magic tricks and get free food, it could cost your family, relationships, all that you have, and even your life. If you were handed keys to a new mansion, you would have to leave your old house to accept the new. Similarly, you have to leave behind your old ways to embrace the new. There are costs; following Jesus is not always easy.

My experience has proved the closer I get to Him, the stronger the temptations. When Jesus was tempted in the wilderness, the temptations grew in size: first bread, then testing God's protection, then an offer of the whole world. If you are not being tempted, then you are not enough of a threat to evil. Consider temptation proof that you are moving in the right direction and evil wants to derail you.

"Consider it pure joy, my brothers and sisters, whenever you face trials of many kinds, because you know that the testing of your faith produces perseverance. Let perseverance finish its work so that you may be mature and complete, not lacking anything." James 1:2-4

So what is the cost? Have you faced difficulty turning from the wrong path, or standing up for what is right, or expressing your faith? Jesus said you must count the cost of following Him and the cost could be great. However, the cost of not following Him is an eternal debt that will never be satisfied. Which one can you afford?

I pray that we would take up our crosses if need be and follow Jesus.

Bleeding in the Darkness

Good Friday. The darkest day of the Christian year. Both dark and light. The darkness of Jesus' suffering and crucifixion and the light of knowing Sunday is on the way, that the grave could not conceal Him. I often wonder about Peter and John, who did not know what was coming. In our church, it is customary throughout the service to gradually dim the lights to darkness. I settled in at the piano to lead *Were You There?* with only the light of a flickering candle on the altar. Then all the lights went out. I had one more piece to sing. I located middle C by shear accident and fumbled through the song. I gained a much greater appreciation for Ray Charles.

I had entered the church feeling prepared, but found I was not. When Jesus was in the garden, Peter said he was prepared to die with Him, but when the time came to stand, he denied that he knew Jesus. Oh, how often have I done the same, only to hear the rooster crow, running out and weeping bitterly because of my failure.

I wondered why my musical offering ended up in the dark. Our pianist did a masterful job playing, in full light with music scattered from side to side. I had to play by heart. Maybe that was the point.

There have been days when I sang in church and stumbled back to my pew, completely spent, as if I spilled my life-blood across the keys, exhausted from spending just a few minutes at the feet of Jesus. Tonight, I knelt at the foot of the cross and somehow, His precious blood intermingled with my own, across a collection of alternating ebony and ivory, light and dark. The burdens I carried were left behind in the darkness of an empty sanctuary, just as Jesus left my sins behind in the grave. *Hallelujah.*

Upon reflection, it seemed the tempo of the earlier songs was a bit too upbeat for the feel of the evening. I played my music slowly and softly and the congregation left in somber silence. I had opened myself up, not to what I had prepared to do, but to what God needed of me. Jesus bled in the darkness that Friday and I was called to figuratively do the same.

I pray that my meager talent was what God needed it to be.

Incessant Prayer

Incessant – continuing without pause or interruption, often regarded as something unpleasant. Unpleasant? Not Always.

I awoke, mind full of struggles that troubled my sleep. Thoughts of what needed to be done and what may not get done, bills that had to be paid and some that may not be so lucky. I spent some quiet time considering prayer without ceasing.

"Rejoice always, pray continually, give thanks in all circumstances; for this is God's will for you in Christ Jesus." 1 Thessalonians 5:16-18

Continually, without pause or interruption, incessantly. God-conversations are a good thing when you can carve a few minutes out of your day. But what about when life comes at you?

We are experts of the multi-task, write with one hand and juggle with the other while carrying on a separate conversation. Perhaps we should use those skills in our prayer life as well. In every situation, keep an ongoing conversation with God; keep asking God what He wants you to say, how can you further His kingdom in this very moment by your words or actions.

Taking a walk this morning with the dog at my heals, the skies were foggy and the warm air stood still as if waiting for something to break the silence. Consumed by worry, I approached God with a bruised heart seeking His direction. He said, *"Lift your eyes and breathe deep."* As I did, a brilliant sunrise peered through the haze, with remnants of morning mist sparkling on the leaves. A peaceful pause and signs of spring all around, my eyes were filled with the beauty I had ignored minutes earlier. As my focus was broken by barrage of messages from colleagues who thought they needed my immediate help, I figured they could wait and let me finish my morning walk with God. Then my phone rang from a friend who had passed away a few years back and it shocked me to see his name on the phone, even though I knew his number had been transferred to someone else, I just hadn't changed my contact info yet. There was no one on the other end. Kind of a heavenly jab that maybe I was on to something.

Pray continually. Do not let the conversation end with "Amen". Lift your eyes and breathe deep. Give thanks in all circumstances for this is God's will for you in Christ Jesus.

Amen ....

Moments of Sabbath

On a bright Sunday morning, I awoke to the soft sounds of silence, the gentle rhythm of my wife sleeping peacefully and the distant rumble of vehicles headed to their early morning destinations. As I scanned the pages of my digital collection of devotionals, sports scores and general foolishness, a message arrived that said, "Get Up, Get Dressed, and Get to Church." I see value in fellowship of community, promoting worship if not actually leading it, and training children in the way they should go, but when it feels like an obligation, church can lose its luster.

Sabbath, or the Hebrew "sabbat", is derived from the verb "sabat", meaning to stop or cease. It is traditionally a representation of the seventh day of creation when God rested.

"Remember the Sabbath day by keeping it holy. Six days you shall labor and do all your work, but the seventh day is a sabbath to the Lord your God. On it you shall not do any work ... For in six days the Lord made the heavens and the earth, the sea, and all that is in them, but he rested on the seventh day. Therefore the Lord blessed the Sabbath day and made it holy." Exodus 20:8-11

Jewish tradition sets the Sabbath day on Saturday. The ancient laws were such that if you did work that day, breaking of the Sabbath was punishable by death; yet Jesus challenged this.

"*On a Sabbath Jesus was teaching in one of the synagogues, and a woman was there who had been crippled by a spirit for eighteen years. When Jesus saw her, he said to her, "Woman, you are set free from your infirmity." Then he put his hands on her, and immediately she straightened up and praised God. Indignant because Jesus had healed on the Sabbath, the synagogue leader said to the people, "There are six days for work. So come and be healed on those days, not on the Sabbath." The Lord answered him, "You hypocrites! Doesn't each of you on the Sabbath untie your ox or donkey from the stall and lead it out to give it water? Then should not this woman, a daughter of Abraham, whom Satan has kept bound for eighteen long years, be set free on the Sabbath day from what bound her?"* Luke 13:10-16

"*Then he said to them, 'The Sabbath was made for man, not man for the Sabbath. So the Son of Man is Lord even of the Sabbath.'* " Mark 2:27-28

Jesus showed that the Sabbath was a time for rest, not an obligation to a law, but as instruction from God to slow down, to not work so hard, and enjoy the gifts that this life offers. Take time to cease, to enjoy, to rest. Christians traditionally observe Sundays as Sabbath. Yet too many consider their "obligation" to spend one hour, dressed in our "Sunday Best", sitting in uncomfortable pews, trying to stay awake during a sermon, mumbling through a few songs, shaking the pastor's hand and heading out to a Sunday lunch. The two extremes have completely missed the point.

The time of rest is "*a sabbath to the Lord*" and the Lord "*made it holy*". If "T*he Sabbath was made for man*" and it is holy, why should it be limited to a Saturday, or an hour on Sunday? If the word "Sabbath" was based on a verb, then it is less a certain day or time, and more of an action. A prayer, a hug, a deep breath when you are in need of some Godly strength. These are truly moments of Sabbath.

When I peer off into the distance, my wife will ask what is going on inside my head. At times, it is a million things, other times, nothing. Taking a walk, a chance to breathe in fresh air, a momentary change of venue or offering a silent prayer for a random person passing by. A smile, acknowledging God's sense of humor at something He sends my way. To put pen to paper as I listen for Heavenly whispers. A chance to love for the sake of love itself. That is how I observe Sabbath.

The Circus

Life is a circus.

Some days are the calm before the storm; dawn has yet to break, the big top is empty, and the animals are beginning to wake from their slumber. Other days seem to be spent sweeping the floors and shoveling out the elephant stalls. But today, I'm riding a unicycle on a tight rope without a net, over three rings of roaring tigers, dancing bears and of course, clowns . . . lots of clowns. As the crowd screams, anticipating some grand gesture, I try to catch a trapeze to swing gracefully from one task to another, if that were only possible.

"No one can serve two masters. Either you will hate the one and love the other, or you will be devoted to the one and despise the other. You cannot serve both God and money." Mathew 6:24

The other "master-wanna-be-s" pull me further away from the Master I choose to serve, Almighty God. With clowns to the left of me, jokers to the right, I take a deep cleansing breath and pray the name of "Jesus". I instantly see the craziness through calmed eyes. Incessant whining fades to a bearable level as I step outside the big top to see the sun is just as bright and the air is just as clear.

I need to keep my eyes on Jesus, not just for direction but also empowerment. He will not lead you to a place that He has not equipped you to go. The challenge is keeping my heart in tune with God when the world tries to direct me away. When circus folk surround me, I lose sight of The Ringmaster. When I focus on Him the trained monkeys seem to scatter.

"This is what the Lord says— your Redeemer, the Holy One of Israel: 'I am the Lord your God, who teaches you what is best for you, who directs you in the way you should go. If only you had paid attention to my commands, your peace would have been like a river, your well-being like the waves of the sea.' " Isaiah 48:17-18

Peace like a river.
I long to dive in and float down that river.

Grace Unseen

Early morning walk. A frigid breeze blows through me as the dog finds every smell left behind by nocturnal visitors. Too cold for playtime and I have a big day ahead. Frustration spills over into my quiet time. Forging through the morning routine, in the solace of a warm truck, I pass other weary travelers headed to where Monday morning takes them. This is usually time for prayer and reflection, but not this morning. Traffic is moving and green lights abound. My phone rings with the sweet voice of my dear bride with a change in plans; a welcome distraction from the mundane commute. I see the next green light in the distance turn to yellow. "I can make it" but I have seen too many crack'em-ups at that intersection, so I thought better of it.

The red light was only momentary but it gave pause to consider the interruption. God's hand is in all things, so was this really a random occurrence? Was there impending danger ahead that a small lapse of time prevented?

"Teach me, and I will be quiet." Job 6:24

An excerpt from a different story, but simple and poignant. A chance to stop, be quiet and allow God to teach me.

I try to approach difficulties as a way for God to work in me (or more often, work on me). How many times has my life been spared by His grace that I have not seen?

"For the Lord your God dried up the Jordan before you until you had crossed over. The Lord your God did to the Jordan what he had done to the Red Sea when he dried it up before us until we had crossed over. He did this so that all the peoples of the earth might know that the hand of the Lord is powerful and so that you might always fear the Lord your God." Joshua 4:23-24

Joshua came to a shallow part of the river where waters had to be halted miles upstream to dry up at the crossing. God does not need to manipulate the constraints of this physical world to wield His power, but perhaps He chose to hold back the water hours or even days before the crossing, performing miracles long before Joshua needed it.

How often has God intervened that we avoided dangers unaware? How many times do we encounter a pleasant coincidence, seemingly a result of redirection at every turn? How many unknown journeys have we traveled by the grace of God?

Faith is the belief in the unseen. Grace is the gift of a loving God to we, the undeserving. How much grace have we received that we will not know until we sit at the feet of Jesus and He tells us the story?

I am looking forward to finding out.

Lunch with Jesus

Having lunch at Firehouse Subs where you place your order, they call your name and bring it to you. I was enjoying lunch, lost in my own thoughts, then the man called out, "Order for Jesus!" I looked up in great anticipation to see where he was taking the tray. The recipient clarified that his name was pronounced "Ha-Sus". I grinned at the thought of having lunch with Jesus, but then I thought, "Why not?"

"He said to them: 'It is not for you to know the times or dates the Father has set by his own authority.'" Acts 1:7

So why not walk into a sandwich shop, sit down and share my lunch?

Joseph Girzone wrote a series of novels called *Joshua* about a stranger visiting in a small town. Joshua interacted with the townsfolk, revealing just enough to make you wonder if he could be Jesus. It is a great series of books that leaves you thinking about the possibility of Jesus living among us.

We share a meal at the communion table on

Sundays, so why not a "Dalmatian spotted" lunch table on a Tuesday afternoon? The church is God's house so why can't Firehouse be Jesus' favorite sandwich shop? So I invited the "real" Jesus to have a seat, and we talked. A nice visit discussing the crazy and the mundane. This is the kind of relationship He wants, to be a part of everything, not just an hour on Sunday morning. We talked about my being overwhelmed and unprepared for the tasks ahead. Then He said:

"My grace is sufficient for you, for my power is made perfect in weakness. Therefore, embrace your weakness so that My power may rest on you." 2 Corinthians 12:9

Wow. Good talk, Russ.

I arose with both my belly and heart full, refreshed and ready to take on whatever is next. It is nice to know that He is that close in the ordinary. We just have to ask and listen.

I recommend that you invite Jesus to have a seat and just talk.

Heaping Coals

Fearing an upcoming confrontation that unfortunately happens too often, I prayed for God to help me approach the situation in the best way possible to lessen the impact, to "calm the storm" a bit. His response was, *"forgive him."*

What? Forgive him? Has he actually done anything requiring forgiveness, other than being just a pain in the lower extremities? *"Forgive him."* Forgiveness is not always for the other person as much as for ourselves. Whether it was a true wrong or a perceived wrong, it still had a grip on me.

"If your enemy is hungry, give him food to eat; if he is thirsty, give him water to drink. In doing this, you will heap burning coals on his head, and the Lord will reward you." Proverbs 25:21-22

Yeah, heap burning coals, I'll forgive him, that'll show him. *"Uh, No. That's not what that means and that's not how I taught you."*

When this proverb was written, if during the night your fire went out, you would go ask a neighbor for a hot coal to restart your fire. The proverb was about being generous, giving not just one coal, but all they could carry, in a pot, most likely carried on their head. Thus, a heap of coals on the head.

Forgiveness is a gift, just as it is a gift to us from God. So if I forgive, then I'm the bigger person right? If they no longer have power over me, then I have power over them, right? *"Uh, no. That's not how I taught you."*

A discussion came to mind from the book *The Shack* by William P. Young. God was asking the main character to forgive the man that killed his daughter. When he protested, God said He needed him to, though it may take a thousand times before it was easier. God wanted to redeem the other man, too.

Jesus did not die for us to prove He was better than we were; He already was and still is. He did it because He loves us. He wants me to forgive because He loves all of us and is trying to redeem all His children. He paid our ransom asking nothing in return, but only to go and do the same.

Talk about heaping coals on my head.

So I said, "I forgive him", and again, and again. Only 997 more to go.

Fork in the Road

Traveling along my own merry way, a pothole seemed to take the air out of my tires. Plans for a long weekend at the beach did not turn out as planned, in fact, quite the opposite. A thought came to mind that God leaves the toughest battles to the strongest warriors. Now there are certainly harder battles than a vacation gone wrong and surely greater warriors than I. Besides, the vacation was not "Clark Griswald" bad. The more we pressed on, the more went wrong, a comedy of errors before our very eyes. Frustrated and a bit angry, I stumbled off my path. My morning devotional was about being a generous giver and not worrying about money. That, of course, made me feel convicted about my giving (or lack thereof) and made me worry about money. My disgust turned to apathy. I decided to spend a few dollars on a lotto dream of great riches (not surprisingly it did not turn out as I hoped). I thought, "Why not? It's just a couple of bucks." That led to, "Why not? It's just a few extra calories". Areas that I have been struggling with fell behind the mask of "Why nots". Moreover, the beach provided too many opportunities for my eyes to wander, not a good place for "why not?"

As I continued farther away, I came to a point where I could continue to slide down the slippery slope or turn around and right the ship; a fork in the road. Then a scripture came to mind.

"But if serving the Lord seems undesirable to you, then choose for yourselves this day whom you will serve, whether the gods your ancestors served beyond the Euphrates, or the gods of the Amorites, in whose land you are living. But as for me and my household, we will serve the Lord." Joshua 24:15

Whoa, that was loud and clear.
"But as for me and my household, we will serve the Lord."

Each time a tempting opportunity stood in my way, I kept hearing, "choose this day whom you will serve."
"But as for me and my household, we will serve the Lord."

I pray that this scripture continues to echo in my mind as I face what challenges the real world throws at me.

A Nickle's Worth of Grace

The first of the month is looming, time to dive into the pile of bills on my desk, not my favorite task. Anxiety arises, wondering if the journey will be an uphill climb, relatively flat trek, or hopefully, a downhill, feet-off-the-pedals, ride.

"Two things I ask of you, Lord; do not refuse me before I die: Keep falsehood and lies far from me; give me neither poverty nor riches, but give me only my daily bread. Otherwise, I may have too much and disown you and say, 'Who is the Lord?' Or I may become poor and steal, and so dishonor the name of my God." Proverbs 30:7-9

We pray, *"Give us today our daily bread." Matthew 6:11.* No more, no less (though a little more would be nice). My wavering faith had me wondering if the bread would leaven enough to make a larger loaf.

"But so that we may not cause offense, go to the lake and throw out your line. Take the first fish you catch; open its mouth and you will find a four-drachma coin. Take it and give it to them for my tax and yours." Matthew 17:27

The bible tells us Peter payed the temple tax with a coin found in a fish's mouth. Of all the fish he could have caught, Peter reeled in the one with the exact amount they needed for the tax. (Scholars argue whether the fish had simply swallowed the shiny object, or the Lord made the coin appear there. Either way, it was awesome.) The underlying point is that Peter did something unusual, at Jesus' leading, without knowing the outcome, and the Lord provided. Therefore, continue to pursue where the Lord is leading, even if you cannot see it bearing fruit. The Lord will provide.

    I started separating the few "ins" from all the "outs". There was just enough month at the end of the money, except for one surprising need in the amount of $150. I will have to be creative and something has to wait. Pondering my options, I opened the other miscellaneous mail that tends to overtake the mailbox and found an unexpected refund check for $150.05. Just the coin in the fish's mouth I needed.

    Every bill was paid with a nickel to spare. I did pray for my daily bread, no more, no less, and that a little more would be nice; and a little more was given. I am grateful and blessed. If you look at that nickel, it says "In God We Trust". I do not trust Him as much as I should, but a nickel's worth of grace was a great reminder.

    Whether five cents or five million, be grateful for what God provides.

Crumbs

" 'First let the children eat all they want,' he told her, 'for it is not right to take the children's bread and toss it to the dogs.' 'Lord,' she replied, 'even the dogs under the table eat the children's crumbs.' Then he told her, 'For such a reply, you may go; the demon has left your daughter.' She went home and found her child lying on the bed, and the demon gone." Mark 7:27-30

    A difficult passage for me; this woman was not Jewish and it seemed that Jesus had insulted her because of her lineage. The Greek word for "dog" used in this verse did not refer to the "dirty, roaming the streets" kind of dog, but of an "inside, little dog", a puppy endeared by the children and the master of the house. To "toss" the bread to a puppy was a treat that would come before the regular supper time. Either way, the woman acknowledged her place as "not a child of Israel."
    From what this woman had heard of Jesus, her request would take just a word from His lips to heal her daughter, simply a "crumb" of His power. When Jesus saw her faith, even that of a

Gentile, He granted her request. But the story doesn't end there. Not only did she believe that a "crumb" from Jesus would be enough, she turned to leave, believing the healing was done. Faith in approaching, faith in asking and faith that she would receive.

Often I have felt like the dog under the table, sniffing at the bounty above, hoping for a morsel to fall my way. Many have been blessed in great abundance, some by the sweat of their own brow, others, not so much. I too have been blessed with a bowl-full at supper time, yet an extra crumb or two would be welcomed. I have stood on my hind legs pretending to belly up to the grownup table, only to lose my balance, return to all fours and expose my masquerade. Humble pie is a dish served cold and it sticks in the throat.

"Don't think you are better than you really are. Be honest in your evaluation of yourselves, measuring yourselves by the faith God has given us." Romans 12:3 NLT

I should measure myself by the faith God has given me, the place He has led me, and the things He has led me to and through.

The woman in the story accepted her station as not worthy to sit at the table. She did not ask for the whole loaf, but only a crumb. She returned home to find that a "crumb" was more than enough.

Seek only the crumbs of blessings. You may receive the entire loaf.

Of Dreams and Dog Toys

   Stumbling through a Monday morning in the dim light of a pre-dawn sunrise, I ran across a pile of chewed-on dog toys. Tattered and a little worn, they lay quiet and deflated, but certainly loved, metaphors in the making. Thoughts of my daughter's bold visions of her future brought back a few of my own when I was her age: make a lot of money, have a nice house and a great family. Well, achieving the latter two out of all three is not too bad.
   Most delusions of grandeur of a foolish young man lay broken and deflated like those dog toys. Shiny when new, they squeaked with delight when squeezed just the right way. Often buried under the tough rawhide of everyday life, they would be chewed on vigorously when the opportunity arose, until the "squeak" turned out to be a piece of plastic, and it's substance was scattered on the floor like the white fluff that hides under the couch and seemingly in every corner.
   Lamenting the excitement and "new toy smell" that has passed, I sought the Father's consult regarding these things.

" 'For I know the plans I have for you,' declares the Lord, 'plans to prosper you and not to harm you, plans to give you hope and a future. Then you will call on me and come and pray to me, and I will listen to you. You will seek me and find me when you seek me with all your heart.' " Jeremiah 29:11-13

"Commit to the Lord whatever you do, and he will establish your plans." Proverbs 16:3

Offer old dreams to the Lord to use as He sees fit, that He may be glorified. The deflated images may still have enough "stank" to make them chewable, yet the Lord can put a shine to them, or use lessons learned to forge new dreams, His plans for you.

Where the Heck am I Going?

At a local pharmacy, I sat next to an older gentleman. We exchanged pleasantries and talked about the weather, as two old coots will do. He said it felt good to sit for a while because he was busier now than before he retired. Considering the day ahead and the giants that awaited me, it is hard to imagine being busier. After completing his purchase, he turned to wish me a good day, and being slightly disoriented in the maze of store shelves, he said, "Oh, where the heck am I going?"

Life has been a struggle between new ideas and the same old tires in the same ruts. Feeling bruised and a bit disoriented myself; I repeated his words, "Oh, where the heck am I going?" A phone call interrupted the mundane silence of people waiting in line and the beeps of cash registers. It appears the Goliaths have found me and are shouting from the distance.

David spent his early days caring for sheep, battling bears, lions and anything else that threatened his flock. When he went to deliver food to his brothers, he heard Goliath taunting his people and his God. Many cowered from the mighty warrior; however, David chose to face him. They dressed him in armor but it was too heavy for his small frame. He opted instead to venture out with what he knew: a sling and a few small stones. The giant laughed, but David knew the battle would not be won by strength or sword, only by the Power of God. One small stone in one small sling from one small boy with the will of God and Goliath fell.

"Then he took his staff in his hand, chose five smooth stones from the stream, put them in the pouch of his shepherd's bag and, with his sling in his hand, approached the Philistine." 1 Samuel 17:40

David "chose smooth stones from the stream", fashioned by many years of water passing over them. Likewise, my "shepherd's bag" has a few small stones shaped by the passing of "Living Water". Rocks of faith, prayer, and the ability to listen for heavenly whispers when I need them most. Facing giants and collapsing under the weight of other people's armor, all I needed was a few small stones and my Father's will.

Perhaps it is not as much "Oh where the heck am I going" as it is "Oh where the heck am I going without the power of the Almighty." Stepping in faith is the difference.

Right in the Margins

In a written letter, the margin is the blank space that frames the text, inside of which is where business is done. Accountants see a margin as the extra left over after the costs have been satisfied. My mother's bible has notes in the margins for the "extras" found by reading between the lines. When there was more than the constraints of the printed page would allow, there were scraps of paper and sticky notes. Inside the margins has its purpose, whether that be effort, finances, or time; space that encompasses the necessities in life, your work to provide a roof over your head, food on the table, and all the other needs of your family. The margins are open areas to be filled with thoughts, dreams, relationships, family time, and time to just be still and listen to God's tender voice; time that brings rest, reflection and refreshment.

"*Jabez cried out to the God of Israel, 'Oh, that you would bless me and enlarge my territory! Let your hand be with me, and keep me from harm so that I will be free from pain.' And God granted his request.*" 1 Chronicles 4:10

"Enlarge my territory" leads many to interpret it as an increase in material wealth. Scholars argue that it is not simply speaking of wealth and prosperity, but also of area of influence where we could expand the impact of God, perhaps speaking or singing to the masses. Other translations use the words "enlarge my borders" which could apply to our "personal borders" or margins. Cry out to God that His hand might be with us, to bless our financial endeavors and our spiritual understanding so we may bless others. Grant us more room in the margins, to live, love and do all the things He has planned for us.

" 'For I know the plans I have for you,' declares the Lord, 'plans to prosper you and not to harm you, plans to give you hope and a future.' " Jeremiah 29:11

He knows the plans for us even when we cannot see them. We should spend less time on our plans and more time seeking His. More time in the margins, in prayer and communication with the Almighty Creator that longs to hear our every prayer and helps us to prosper.

Too Many Metaphors

When putting pen to paper, I start with a thought, a vision or a question. Sometimes, a spoken word catches my attention, other times, an image metaphorically activates my "spidey sense;" there is a lesson in there somewhere. My train of thought travels down a certain set of rails, sometimes with more steam, sometimes less. I press onward until I run across a railroad switch that could send me off on a tangent. Most writers try to avoid these, especially if they have a certain storyline or thesis statement to adhere to. I prefer to take a long look down the tangent track in pursuit of creativity or perhaps a touch of wisdom. Often times, a random turn of a phrase can spark too many metaphors to chase. Once I have chosen a direction, I store the other paths in my knapsack to pursue in future journeys.

As metaphors awake my muse, it occurred to me that much of Jesus' teaching was in parables, a series of metaphors. Jesus told stories about God's love and grace in ways that everyone could relate to, regardless of station or background. Explanation was left to interpretation so that the message could be understood as the Spirit allowed. Scholars dig deeper and over-analyze while children learn how to love through Sunday school bible stories. I fall somewhere in-between, blessed with opportunities to see Jesus' teachings in everyday life, which I think is His intent. I welcome metaphors to ponder and tangents to explore. It can be difficult to regain focus of the question at hand, but often I have found the answers I seek are not always where I was looking. Many times, I have found God in places and faces I did not expect.

Un-Train My Heart

"Don't practice until you get it right. Practice until you can't get it wrong." Unknown

    Reinforce muscle memory so that your instinct takes over and your body reacts without a thought. If done correctly, it can be a valuable skill for an athlete; manifesting itself as an outstanding jump shot or a devastating collection of bad habits. The same could be said of our heart muscle. A child is born with the ability to love and can make friends with anyone. Effects of our surroundings teach us to love or hate, determine friend or foe, to respect or despise. Our hearts were created to love, but have been trained to hurt, to fear, or to revisit convenient sins, out of pain, fatigue or sheer apathy. There is heart muscle memory, both good and bad, but in the process of training the good, we must un-train the bad.
    Anything you see becomes a forever-retained memory. Nevertheless, just as the color has faded from my hair, so have memories, only to reappear in the midst of troubled sleep. The point remains; be careful what you see. You will

breathe out what you breathe in. A battle rages between the ears, but remember: It only takes one letter to change "repeat" to "repent".

The Lenten season is traditionally a 40-day period of fasting, reminiscent of Jesus' 40 days in the wilderness before beginning His ministry. It is a time of self-reflection and sacrifice, honoring the sacrifice of Jesus for our sins. *Hallelujah.*

Do not wait for Easter to make a change, commit time to reflect, not just the burden of giving up a bad habit, but instill a new habit. Capture every thought and see if it leads you to the place God wants you to be. Carve out time to read each day. Take time to create. Enjoy the sunrise and ponder great thoughts. Change the radio station, or turn it off completely and use your commute to commune with God. Pray as you fall asleep and pray as you wake.

Training takes commitment and hard work. Un-training takes just as much if not more. The result in both cases is worth the effort.

Martha Moments

A springtime chill permeated predawn hours as I stumbled to a quiet place to prepare for the day. The morning began with God saying, *"Trust Me, do not be afraid. If you are shaken, hold My hand and look for the challenge, the chance to grow."* With an ominous foreshadowing of what may stand in my way, I rubbed sleepy eyes and set my shoulders for the heavy load. Self-laid plans and expected victories quickly changed course leading me into uncharted waters. Trimming sails and battling crashing waves left me battered, realizing that I had not set my anchor deep enough. Finding safe harbor, I sought out a place to close weary eyes and breathe in the quiet of peaceful rest.

Awakened from my slumber by disturbing sounds of panic, I wondered how it may affect the ones I love and those I do not know. Of the growing litany of concerns I carry, I fail to place them at the feet of the Almighty, the One who is really in control. Why do I struggle to carry these burdens when help is just a prayer away? As my apathy broke and I approached the throne of Grace, my laundry list of worry grew longer with each thought, one prayer forward and two prayers back. In the midst of my rambling, a voice echoed:

" 'Martha, Martha,' the Lord answered, 'you are worried and upset about many things, but few things are needed—or indeed only one. Mary has chosen what is better.' " Luke 10:41-42
"But seek first his kingdom and his righteousness, and all these things will be given to you as well." Matthew 6:33

Confidence in knowing God is in control can lull my prayer life into numbness. Is praying, "Thy will be done" enough? Is it lack of faith to keep asking for the same thing when we do not get an answer (or the answer we want)? Can persistent prayer change God's mind or the timing of His will? Perhaps. God loves His children, so who am I to question whether He would move mountains for us? A doctor said taking vitamins could be beneficial as the body will absorb what it needs and discard the rest. In the same way, prayers that already have answers need not be answered again (unless I did not listen the first time). Even in repetitive prayers, we honor God by acknowledging that He alone can answer them. Devotional time, though seemingly fruitless, opens my mind to the voice of God, for something He needs me to hear.

We all have "Martha Moments" scurrying about, trying to please others. However, we must balance "Martha Moments" with "Mary Moments", sitting at the feet of Jesus and listening to Him speak.

Choose your "Moments" carefully

Of Poets and Prophets

"Two roads diverged in a wood, and I —I took the one less traveled by, And that has made all the difference." - Robert Frost

"This is what the Lord says: 'Stand at the crossroads and look; ask for the ancient paths, ask where the good way is, and walk in it, and you will find rest for your souls.'" Jeremiah 6:16

The footsteps of poets and prophets tend to follow the same road. The ancient paths, the good ways where you find peace are too often the least traveled.

A temporary pause in the chaos allowed a rare escape to where the sand was warm and salty air brushed softly across my furrowed brow. In this quiet spot, my worries washed away as tiny shells pulled out to sea by the ebb and flow of undulating waves. The ocean considers my sweat insignificant compared to its vast expanse. Likewise, my momentary struggles are no more than a blink in the eternity God holds in His hand. Arriving at this oasis, I was in need of a change of pace, a refocused direction, finding my center. Peering at the horizon gave pause to consider a bigger picture, God's view. Retracing recent steps, I discovered crossroads I had passed, not recognizing alternate paths. Some were grown over due to lack of footsteps, while I continued in muddy tracks of well-trodden trails.

So tightly wound with the business of the day, I allow my left brain dominance to drown out the call of the creativity that burns in my soul, a passion that uncovers pathways to God's higher ways. Searching for the narrow path less traveled, pondering what is good and Holy, I yearn to spend time in God's presence, not handing Him a laundry list of "my" wants and supposed needs, but simply enjoying each other's company.

Facts and figures line the pathway like berries providing needed sustenance; however, I should not allow the bushes to impede my steps. As I travel, they fade into the distance; memories of mountains that now seem like molehills. At the end of my journey, I will look back over the turns in the road, the potholes where I stumbled, the ditches I fell into and the Lord's footprints where He pulled me out of the mire. I will stand in the company of angels at His feet and I pray I will hear Him say, "Well done, my child."

This is the path I choose to follow, that of poets and prophets, laboring here with heaven in mind. All else is time wasted if not focused on the goal instead of the dust beneath my feet.

Facing crossroads. Praying to find the way of peace, of holiness, of the path less traveled.

Listen to Silence

As poet, author or lyricist, a word-smith relies on the turn of a phrase to express the rhythm of his heartbeat; yet streams of literary consciousness run dry, with pen in hand, an empty page yearning for ink spots, and . . . nothing.

A dear friend, my brother in Christ and in so many others ways had asked for prayer for his great love. Without hesitation, her name was lifted into the Almighty hands of God, for whatever the situation. A few days later, thoughts of her came to mind and I found that she had passed from the hands of Jesus into the arms of Jesus, and my brother was broken. Searching for words to say, I realized I was broken as well. "Sorry-s", condolences, prayers; none seemed sufficient. I sat in silence, staring into the darkened distance.

When my words fail, I lean on the words of God.

"The Lord is close to the brokenhearted and saves those who are crushed in spirit." Psalm 34:18

" 'Lord,' Martha said to Jesus, 'if you had been

here, my brother would not have died. But I know that even now God will give you whatever you ask.' Jesus said to her, 'Your brother will rise again.' Martha answered, 'I know he will rise again in the resurrection at the last day'. Jesus said to her, 'I AM the resurrection and the life. The one who believes in me will live, even though they die; and whoever lives by believing in me will never die.' " John 11:21-27

All appropriate in the situation, but a bit too effortless to send a bible reference in response and say, "read it." This wonderful young lady deserved more. Again, words of God come to mind:

"In the same way, the Spirit helps us in our weakness. We do not know what we ought to pray for, but the Spirit himself intercedes for us through wordless groans. And he who searches our hearts knows the mind of the Spirit, because the Spirit intercedes for God's people in accordance with the will of God." Romans 8:26-27

We were made to dwell in heavenly places and we grieve because we are but square pegs in a room full of round holes, trying to fit in where we do not belong. Our dear ones have finished their race, magnificent journeys that we should celebrate, like bumper stickers showing miles run in a marathon. We continue to run, still seeking our finish line.

"*The Spirit helps us in our weakness and Jesus IS the resurrection and the life.*" This we know and our dear ones are saving a seat for us at the feet of Jesus.

My words may fail, but the Word of God rings true when I stop to listen to silence.

A Boy and His Sack Lunch

A permission slip and a sack lunch. What a great memory. It meant we were getting out of school for a field trip to the museum, or the zoo, or for those of you who grew up around San Antonio, a trip to the Buttercrust Bakery; Ooh, I can still smell the freshly baked bread as we hurried through the tour to get our sample loaf.

The Gospel of Matthew tells of five thousand men, besides women and children who were hungry.

> "It was late so Jesus said, 'Give them something to eat.' Philip answered him, 'It would take more than half a year's wages to buy enough bread for each one to have a bite!' " John 6:7

The disciples found a boy with five loaves of bread and two fish. His "sack" lunch. Jesus had everyone sit; He gave thanks for the food and began to share it. When they were all fed, Jesus said, *"Gather the pieces that are left over. Let nothing be wasted."* John 6:13

They gathered up twelve baskets of leftovers.

Too often my bank account feels merely like lunch money when a multitude of bills are gathering. I am thankful for what I have and it always seems to satisfy the need, though there are not always twelve baskets of leftovers afterward, but in the hands of Jesus, handfuls become basketfuls.

In certain seasons, I am blessed with the ability to weave a few words together and if the wind is blowing just right, a melody or two may come along; my "sack lunch" of sorts. I am the boy with five loaves and two fish. I offer up the little that I have to be used as Jesus' sees fit. I pray my songs, my stories, and most importantly, all that I am, be blessed and multiplied, whether to feed the five thousand or simply for the one soul that needs to hear it today.

Lay what you have at Jesus' feet.

Be the boy with a sack lunch to offer.

God in the Snow Chains

Researching a new venture or perhaps just an expansion of my current journey, the excitement of a new opportunity flooded my mind like a late night TV sales pitch. I retreated to the prayer garden in my heart and asked God that if this was just a passing fancy, please open my eyes to it. I do not want to walk this way alone. His response?

"My Child: 'be sure of this: I am with you always, even to the end of the age.'" Matthew 28:20

Finding myself stuck in a familiar rut, I am considering expanding the width and breadth of my comfort zone, eyeing a wider horizon. There are times when it is wise to follow another's footsteps. In a dense fog, you follow the taillights of the driver in front of you to keep centered. On a snow-covered highway, it is best to keep in the tire tracks of one before you, preferably a large truck that has compacted the snow, allowing better traction. The thought of venturing across a field of freshly drifted snow is exciting, but only if you are equipped with big tires and four-wheel drive. Similarly, when our eyes focus on a new greater adventure, the snow tires are knowledge and the four-wheel drive is equipped through prayer. At some point, you are emboldened to get a little mud on the tires and head out onto the path less traveled. Yet even with prayer and preparation, you can find yourself buried up to the axles before you remember that your toolbox includes a set of snow chains. Strapped around the tires, they create additional traction to guide you out of the sloppy mixture of snow and mud, up to firmer ground.

As we continue our journeys, whether grand or simply rising with the sun to face another day, let us equip ourselves with prayer, knowledge and grateful hearts. Be willing to face the road less traveled, knowing that "God is in the Snow Chains".

Heart First

My precious bride spent many years working in a funeral home, sharing in sadness of her extended family, internalizing aching hearts that can overwhelm a loving soul like hers; it was her ministry. The deceased were but empty shells, yet still a father or mother, son or daughter, friend or foe, deserving dignity, modesty and respect. Her compassion brought comfort in otherwise empty days; with each phone call, day or night, leaving one family to serve another, approaching each saddened room heart first, giving hugs and drying tears.

"Jesus said to another man, 'Follow me.' But he replied, 'Lord, first let me go and bury my father.' Jesus said to him, 'Let the dead bury their own dead, but you go and proclaim the kingdom of God.'" Luke 9:59-60

In her own special way, she was blessed with the strength to do both.

Over our years, we have encountered many doctors, some with good bedside manner, others, not so much. One doctor was so gruff, I demanded to speak to the head of the hospital department, not knowing that we just had seen him. After learning my wife had lived with her maladies longer than he had been treating them, the relationship improved, but not much. There have been a select few that had it not been for them, this beautiful soul would not have survived to become my better half. Those doctors entered exam rooms heart first, emulating the Greatest Healer.

"When Jesus landed and saw a large crowd, he had compassion on them and healed their sick." Matthew 14:14

During the pandemic, there was an outpouring of appreciation for those on the front lines, and deservedly so, dedicating long days away from family and friends; a multitude of warriors who led heart first into the fear of the unknown, regardless of what stood before them or what they left behind.

In all three examples, I have seen the healing touch of Jesus, whether physically, spiritually or both. I am grateful for those who are blessed with the strength to jump in heart first. I strive to be more like them.

Onward and Upward. Heart First.

Reflections in Yellow

Struggling through a midweek business day, my efforts appeared to return fruitless. Experience reminded me gray skies are cyclical. In the midst of an election season, an uneasy society and a volatile economy, forecasting short-term future is a roll of the dice. My supposed intellect tried to explain it away, but my heart disagreed with my head ... again.

When differing factions compete in a tug of war, seeking to capture the banner of truth, I rely on the real Truth, the words of Jesus.

"No good tree bears bad fruit, nor does a bad tree bear good fruit." Luke 6:43
"Thus, by their fruit you will recognize them." Matthew 7:20

Am I producing good fruit? Am I furthering God's kingdom? Do my efforts glorify Him? Business is a necessity to provide for my family and all those that rely on a ob done well. I prayed that God would reveal some balance between math-elete and musician, spreadsheets and the written word.

Storm clouds gathered in a gray sky; a reflection of the state of my soul. Peering up I spotted a single bird resting on a wire while others rode the breeze overhead. Creation is singing songs to me. The radio echoed words about trusting God when mountains are not moving. I took a troubled pause to inhale. Traveling further, I realized the last three traffic lights had turned yellow as I approached the intersections, yet continued through. As the fourth changed from green, I slowed to a stop.

I had asked for clarity, yet did not listen for an answer, so it flashed in yellow. "proceed with caution".

Do not rush through the warning signs or you will reach a stop, either by your own decision or by another more damaging force. God may move mountains as He chooses, in an instant or thousands of years, for each is the same for Him. Jesus taught us to ask and wait for an answer, knock and watch for the door to open, trust and be patient.

Heed caution in yellow lights. Be the bird on the wire, content to rest until a cool breeze lifts him to the sky. Labor to produce good fruit and it will sprout in due season.

Slow at yellow lights. Proceed with caution.

Your Second Thousand Miles

There was a commercial where a woman is shown on a split screen. On one side, she chooses a healthy breakfast, on the other side, not so much, lunch with a salad versus a burrito, going to the gym versus just sitting at her desk, climbing into bed versus collapsing into bed. One good decision led to others, as did the bad ones. Likewise, if you slide off your diet a bit, the next time it is easier. Miss your exercise time and before you know it, a missed day turns into a missed week, into a missed month. Break a promise and the next one is easier to break. Let yourself sin "a little" and it grows into bigger ones. It is a slippery slope.

It stands to reason if a small failure leads to larger failures, then a small victory would lead to greater ones. Making the right choice gives you the power to say, "I did that right, so I can do this right also. I resisted that temptation; this one is not much different." Soon enough, you are not only climbing over hills, you are leaping mountains.

It is said that a journey of a thousand miles begins with one step. Easy to say when you look back on a thousand miles. Not as much when you are staring at the first step.

A wealthy man once told me, "Take care of your pennies, the millions will take care of themselves." Likewise, rejoice in the small steps. Before you know it, you are beginning your second "thousand miles."

Blessed are You, Oh Lord, Creator of all things. May Your Voice in thunder and Whisper in wind fill my soul, flow through my fingers and dance across keys; that the *"words of my mouth and this meditation of my heart be pleasing in your sight, Lord, my Rock and my Redeemer." Psalm 19:14*; that those encountered by Your Grace may be lifted.

Thanks for spending time with me.

john g. adams

Coming Soon
Finding Sea Glass
a novella

Other Titles in the *Echoes* Series
Parables, Lessons and *God* Whispers

If you enjoyed *Echoes Interwoven*,
I'd love to hear from you. Your thoughts matter.

Visit *www.LiftedKeys.com* for more stories,
devotionals and inspiration; words entrusted to lift
hearts and warm souls.

Kindly leave a review on Amazon, Goodreads, or
wherever you discovered my books. Your feedback
not only inspires me but helps others find the same
truth I pray you found here.

Thank you for being part of this journey.

Made in the USA
Monee, IL
22 September 2025

25030068R00056